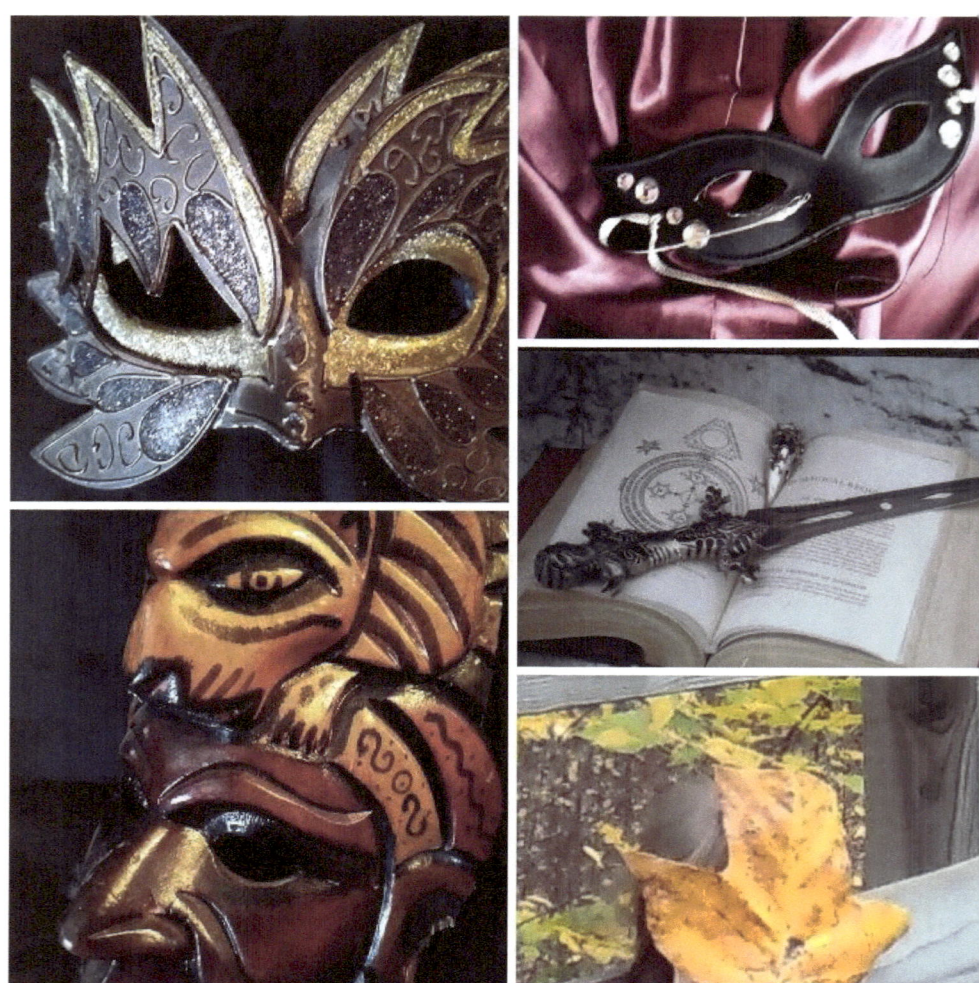

The Many Masks of Magzinnia…
Poetic Revelations

Tina M.E.

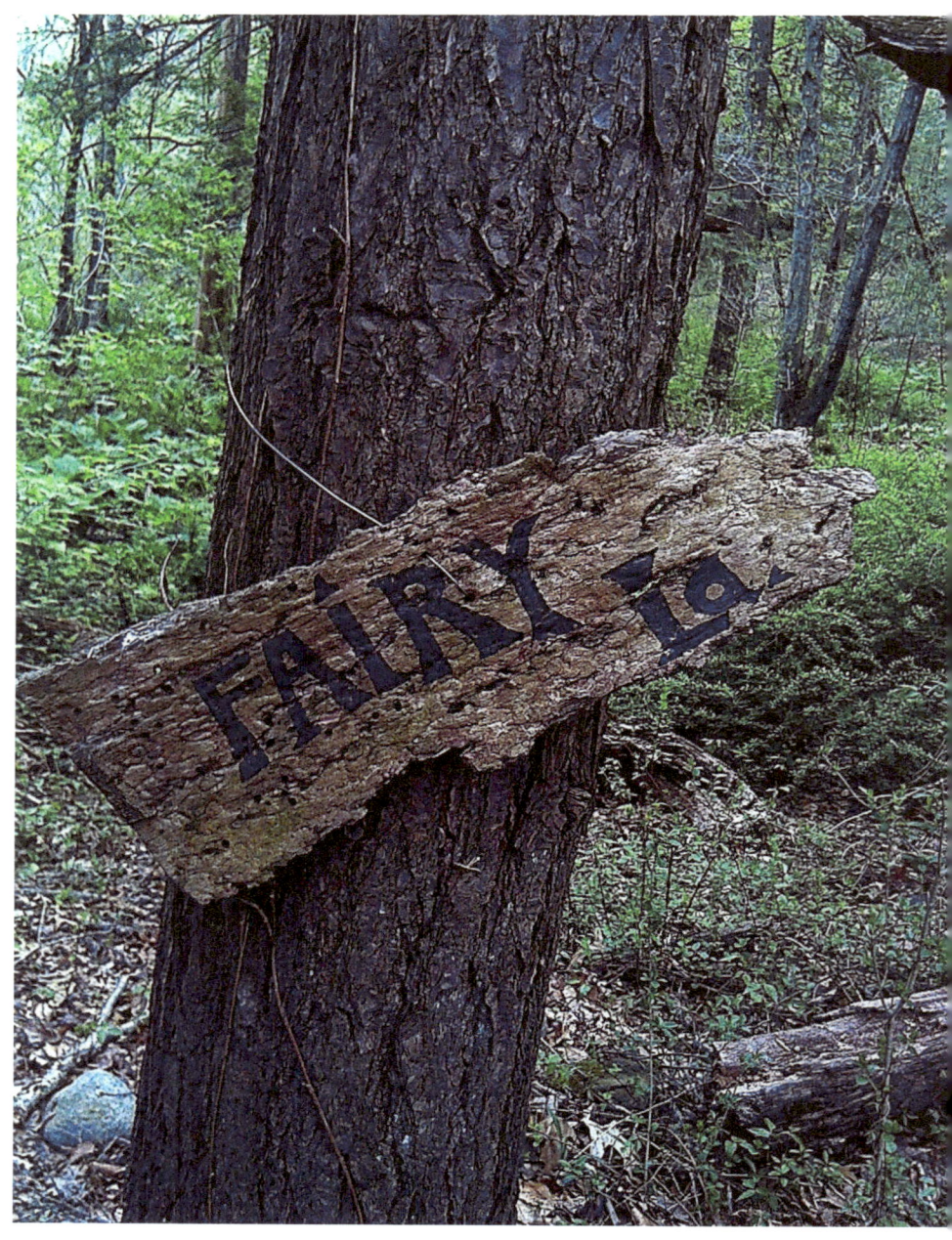

This book is a work of fiction. Names, characters, places and incidents are products of the Author's imagination or are used fictitiously. Any resemblance to actual events or locales or persons, living or dead, is entirely coincidental.

Copyright 2024 Tina M.E.

All rights reserved, including the right to reproduce this book or portions thereof in any form whatsoever.

ISBN -13: 9798612046103

FOLLOW THE AUTHOR:
www.tiktok.com/demondarkfantasy
www.youtube.com/demondarkfantasy
www.tinyindiewhimsy.com
www.instagram.com/tinyindiewhimsy
www.goodreads.com/dantalionofthegoetia

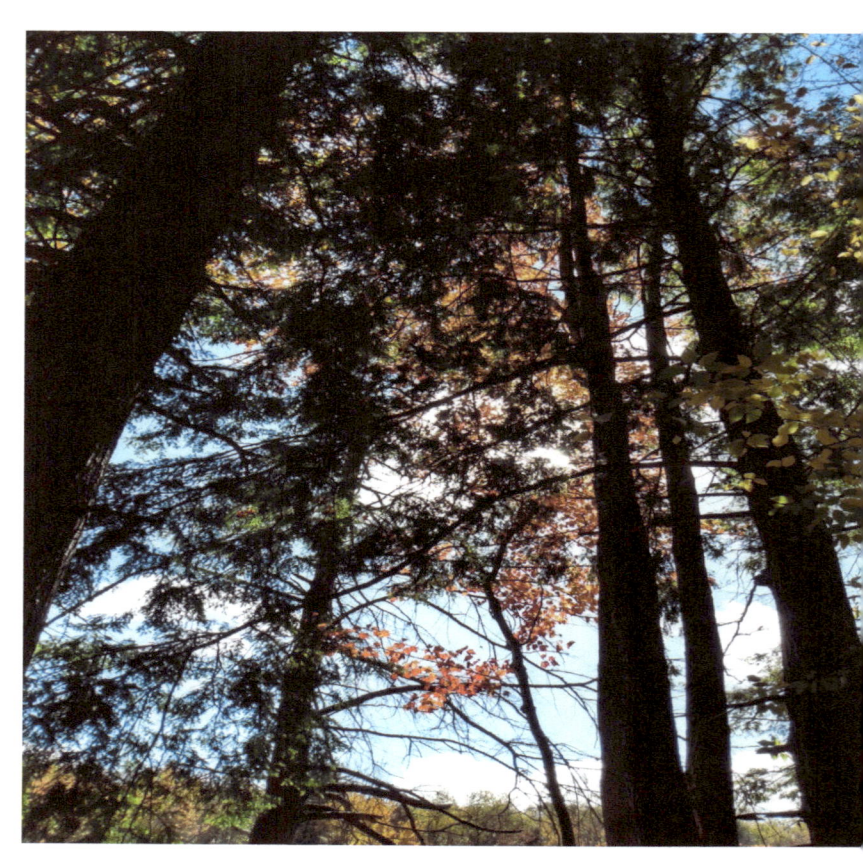

DEDICATION

This Book is dedicated to my daughters…
Who have seen the wearing of many masks
And who have Loved them All…
To their strength and the Power of Three…

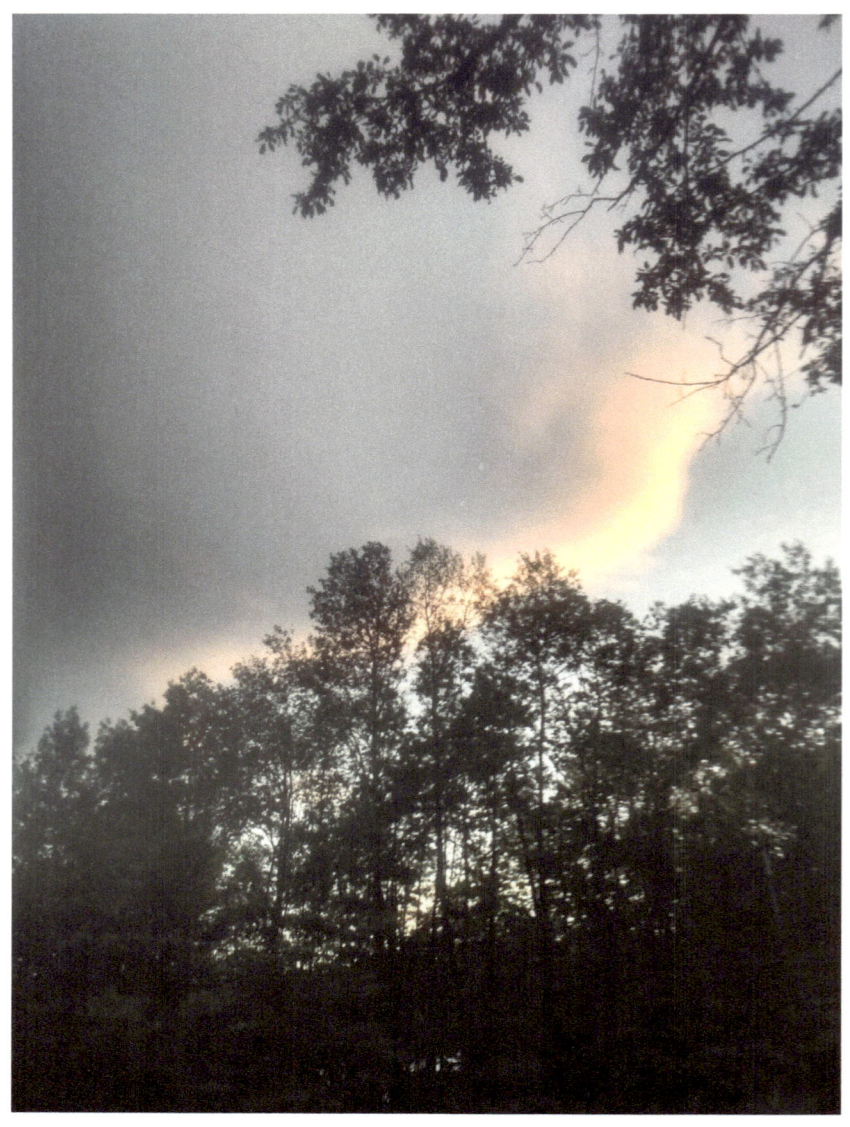

ACKNOWLEDGEMENT

"Heaven wheels above you displaying to you her eternal glories.
And still your eyes are on the ground."

… Dante Alighieri, Italian Poet

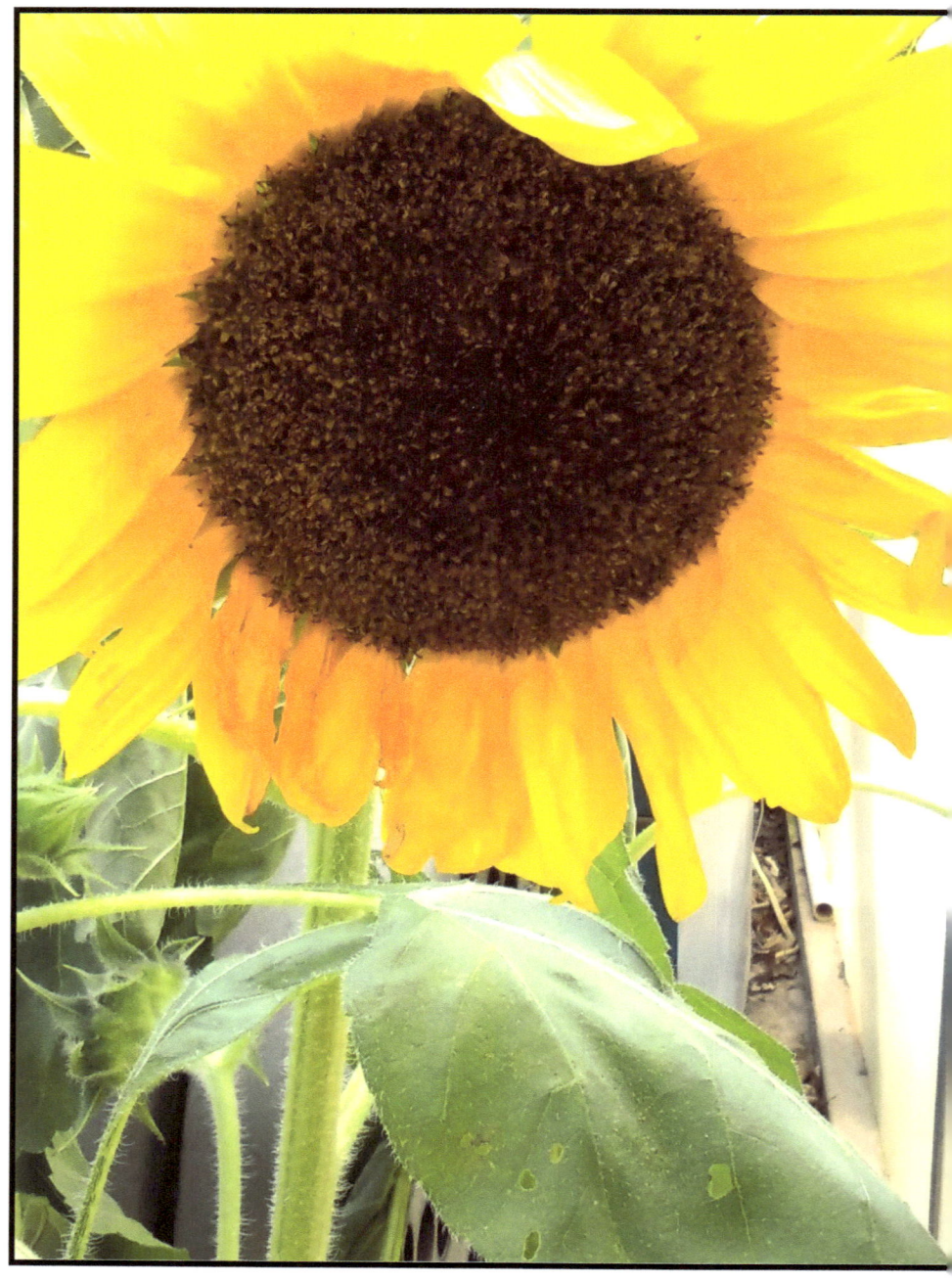

CONTENTS

Poetry

Photography

Poems of Damnation - The Seven Deadly Sinners

Epilogue

Afterward

About The Author

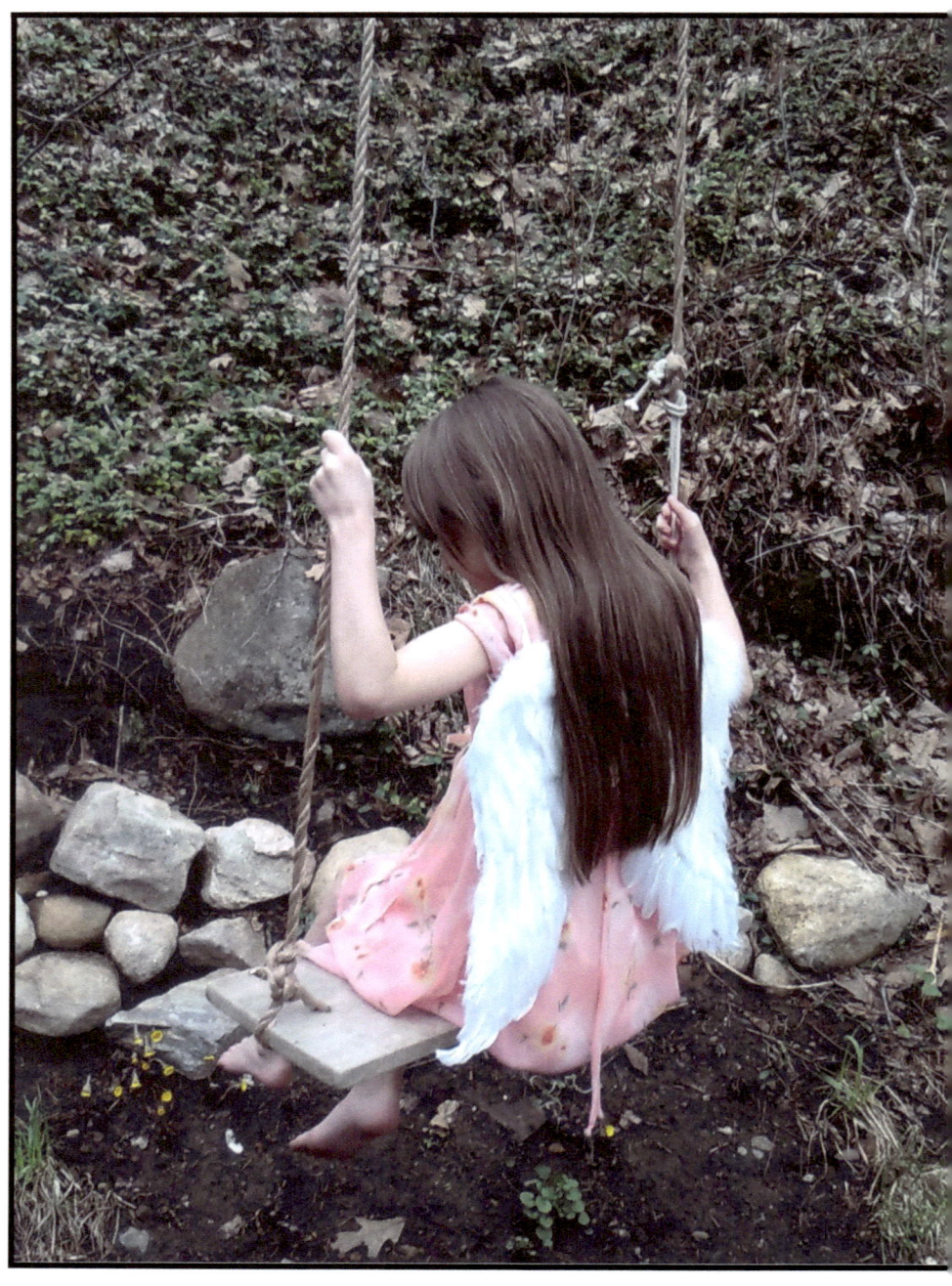

The Many Masks of Magzinnia

She goes by many faces, many masks
Twirling, dancing movements in Autumn's whimsical canvas,
Childlike, fresh and untainted by the torments of humanity
The beating down of one's soul by the familiar and unfamiliar alike,
No, you sweetest Magzinnia,
You wear the Mask of Mercy.
The many guises I wear are unmoving,
They will not be lifted by the wind
But weighted by the mists of time and malevolence,
They are ingrained into my soul
As one sweeping transgression
Which only the Almighty will absolve,
Allowing me to once again wear a new mask
Of tolerance and compassion.

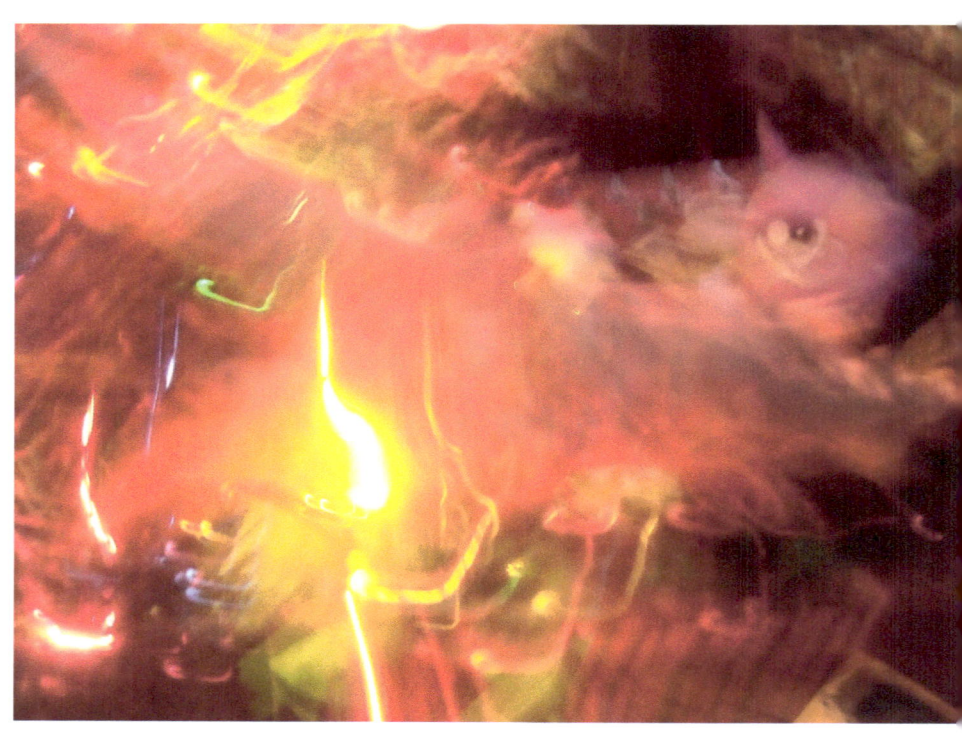

Unveiling The Morning Star

When darkness falls, humans dream.
We, the immortal forgottens ascend the climb towards heaven,
Condemned ourselves, to this Purple Hell of Purgatory bliss,
Where is it leading? What did we miss?
We still have time to count the hours,
Shape our lives upon this tower,
Right our wrongs though bleeding we,
The damned will find eternity
Count every cut and every scar
The blackest pit we've crawled so far,
Into this Hell, unveiling thee.

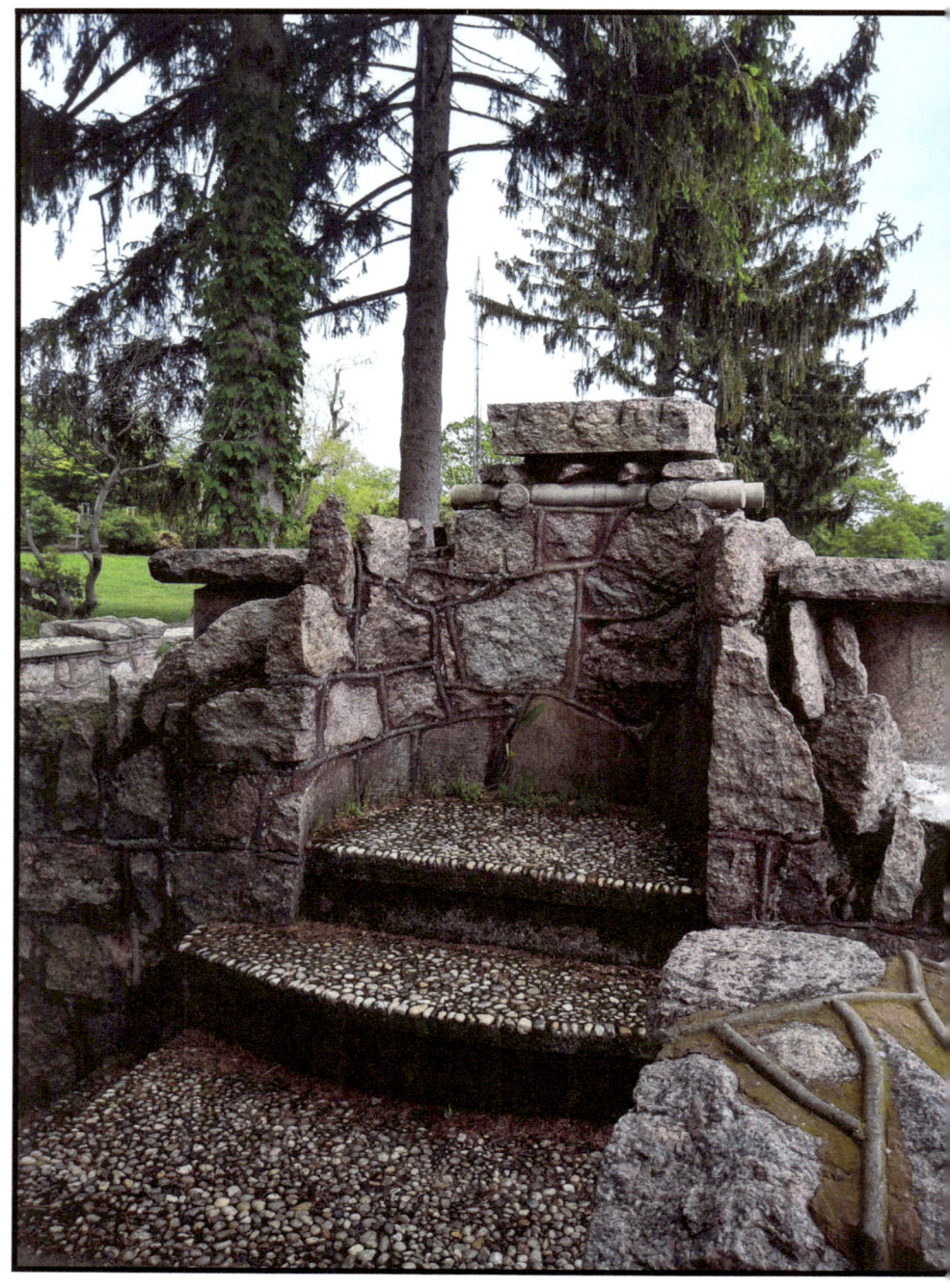

Holy Witch

I inhaled the moon's gaze upon me,
As I touched upon the jagged stone.
I felt my soul emerge through time,
Here to the place I felt so drawn.
It has taken me from the sea to a canopy of green.
I saw my likeness once etched into the stone.
I knew nothing then, yet it was my reflection staring back at me,
Purged of sin only to be thrust into the depths of Hell.
I've come for him above the hill
And beyond the mountain, where are destinies crossed,
Lost, alone, I know, yet I am here.
My soul is ancient, so I must heal from within.
My heart is pure so I must bleed alone.
When I came through the veil I had left everything I once knew behind.
I was the saint and the sinner, the Holy Witch,
Left to the task of making sense of this past life and my place in it.
Taking a diminished soul back into the light of this darkness I had become.

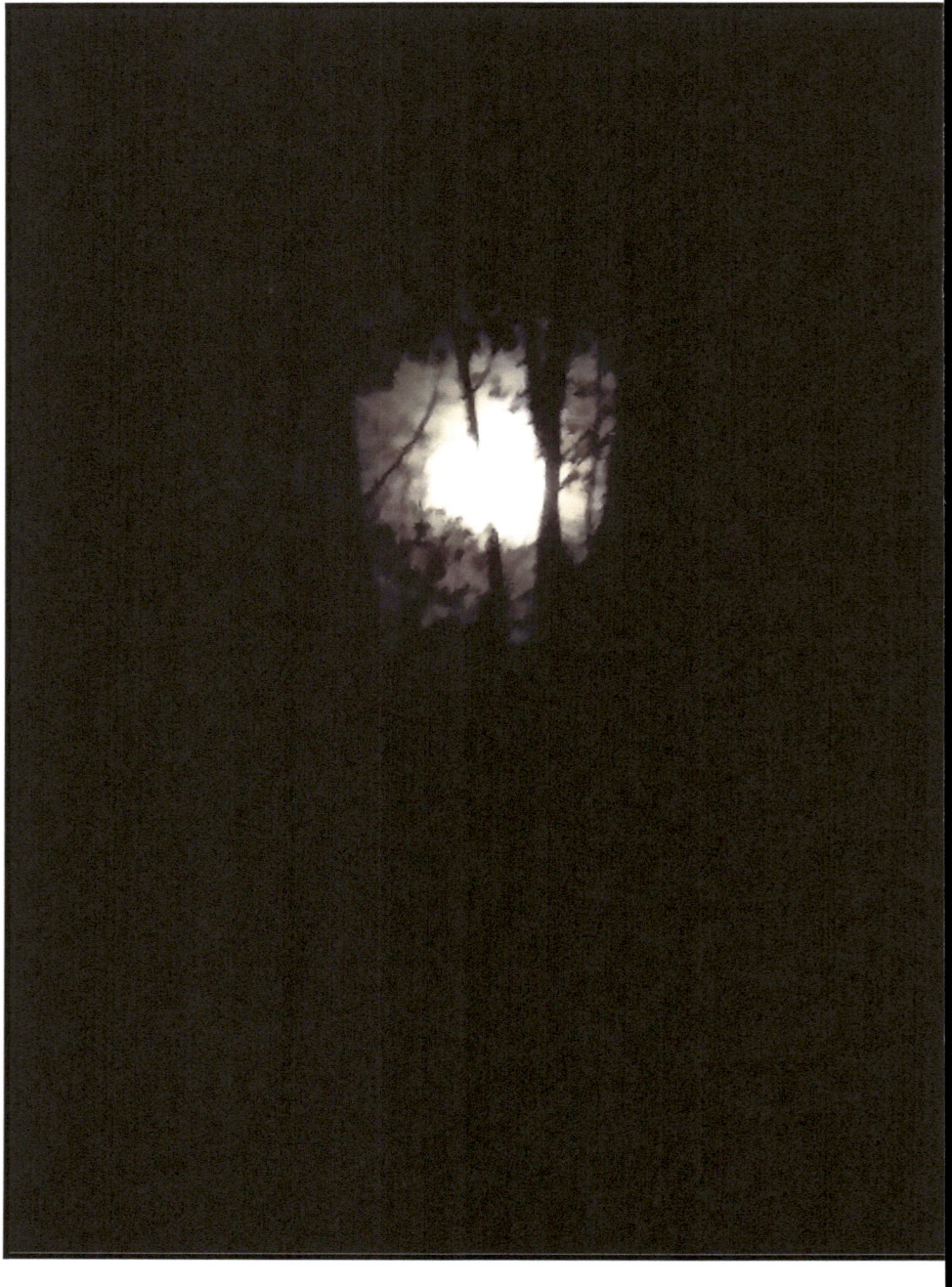

Holy Witch (Continued)

I held the fragile thread of life barely in my grasp.
The tiers of heaven grew higher it seemed,
And I tasted of sin, and witchcraft and sorcery,
And of damnation.
Breathing became a task I forced myself to master.
I found myself back at the tree in the glen,
The memories rushing through my essence.
I wavered, hoping I would recover from the madness.
But it did not go.
I touched upon the pages of the book and began
Writing in words ancient and strange,
Unheard of in my time,
Yet so familiar they filled the parchment with my story.

Redemption

I surrendered love, even life.
You surrounded me,
Wrapped wings, a shroud of protection,
A fragment of hope.
I held true to a distant light that was us.
Within that shroud that was you
I was torn from my light.
Broken from everything that was me,
Your wings let me fall…
Into darkness, into despair,
Into blame… and into hate.
Our demons seal us into our own selves.
False lies unveil the mask that we wear.
Everyone will come to know the answers
Showering the truth down like rain.
I shake off the rain
And move into the light.

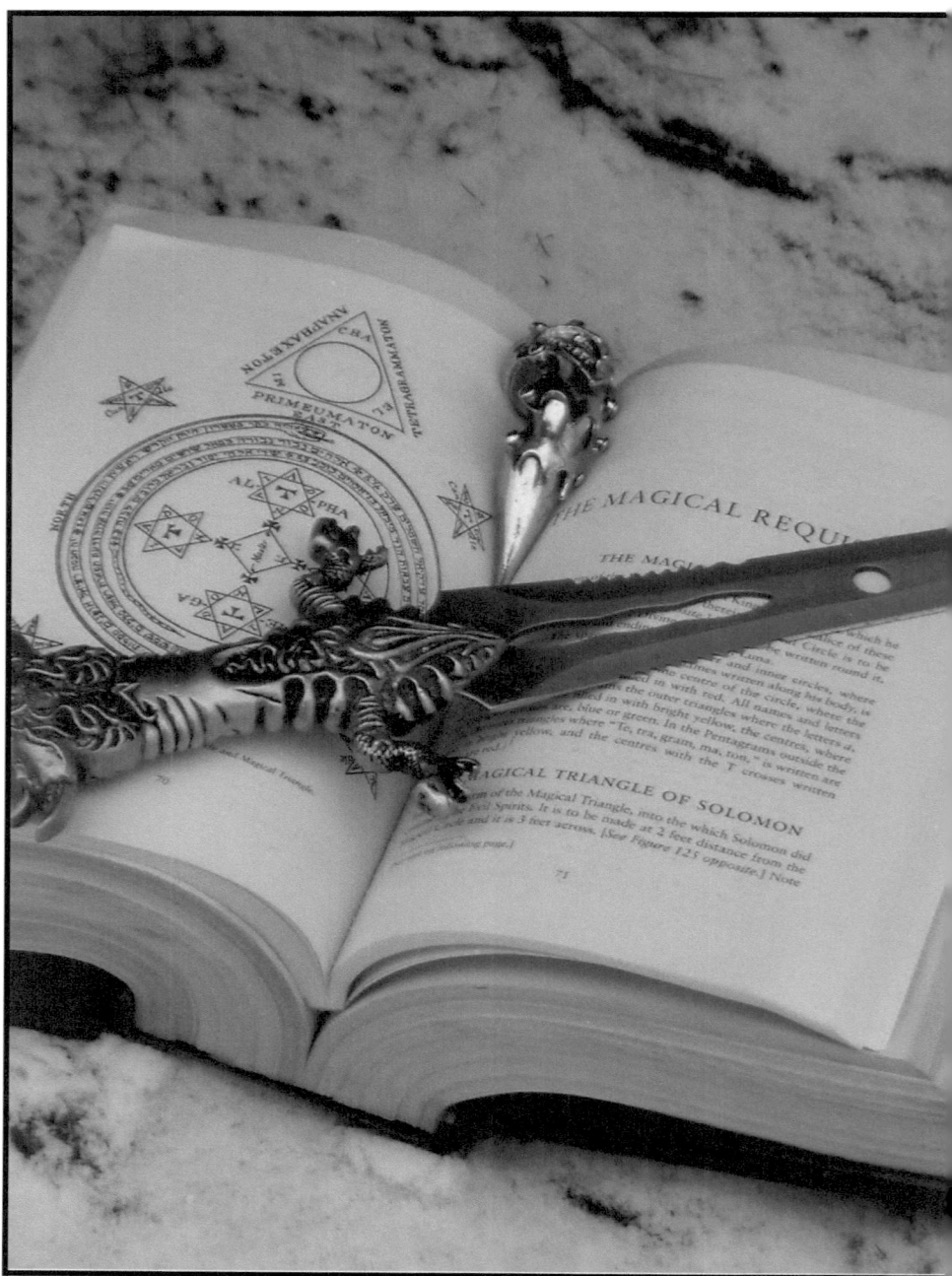

Legacy

The Courtyard slept now…they called the altar "Angel's Tears,"
Faded…forgotten, yet the marks remained.
Deep brands that bind us to our demons.
The damp steady rain washed away every trace
Of Dantalion and Laurel's memory, now only empty, cold stone.
If only the human eye could see.
I stared at the altar, the grimoire off in the distance,
Under the pines, dusted with snow.
I saw her there, innocent, bloodless, alone.
Wisp-like, a memory of something I was supposed to remember.
Every dusk, when the moon was high,
For months I watched as she placed an offering beneath the jagged stone,
Arms and legs outstretched with the moonlight streaming down upon her.
Beautiful, succumbed to the lust of the moon's embrace.
Every mortal sin bled from her soul.
Every single memory pulsed through her,
Every sweetness and every sorrow…
She was to be the Legacy of the grimoire
And I was to bleed for her.

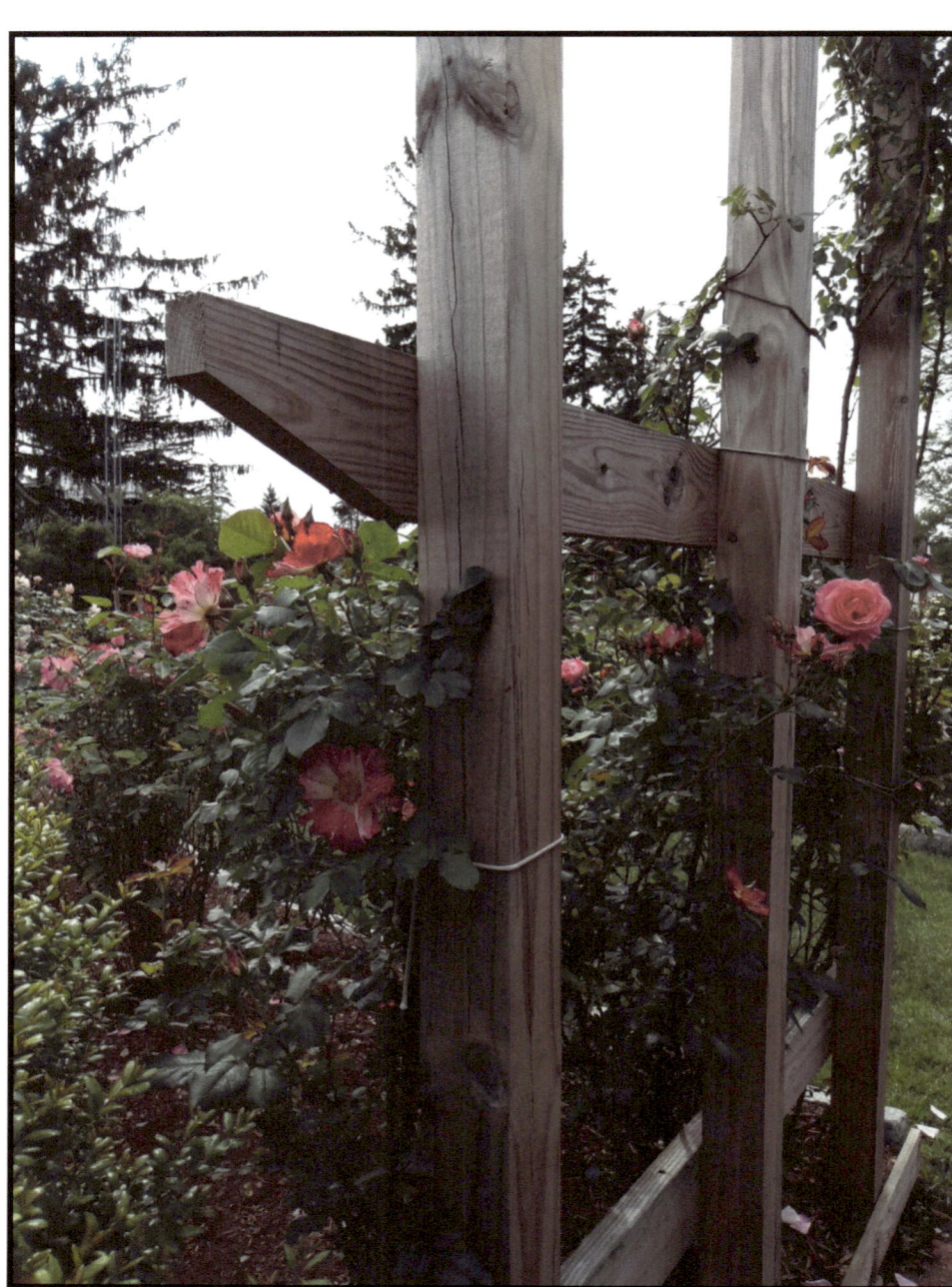

Angel

When all the darkness bleeds from thine eye,
And the only object left of thy gaze therein is light,
Was it then God embraced thy soul in everlasting peace,
Washing away thy sin?
Sinners are we all of this life, wherein we do profess
What seems almost eternal the promise thy will walk
Only toward His light,
Yet darkness calls, tempting us unto jagged pathways of life,
Places thou must go if only to remind us we are but misled,
Bequeathed a broken promise of eternal light.
Yet it is there, at that moment,
Where thine eye gazes upon the brilliance of an Angel
Meant to wrap her Holy wings around thy soul
Warming thy spirit like the sun and washing over the heart
The misty rain of forgiveness,
The true Eternal light of Love…

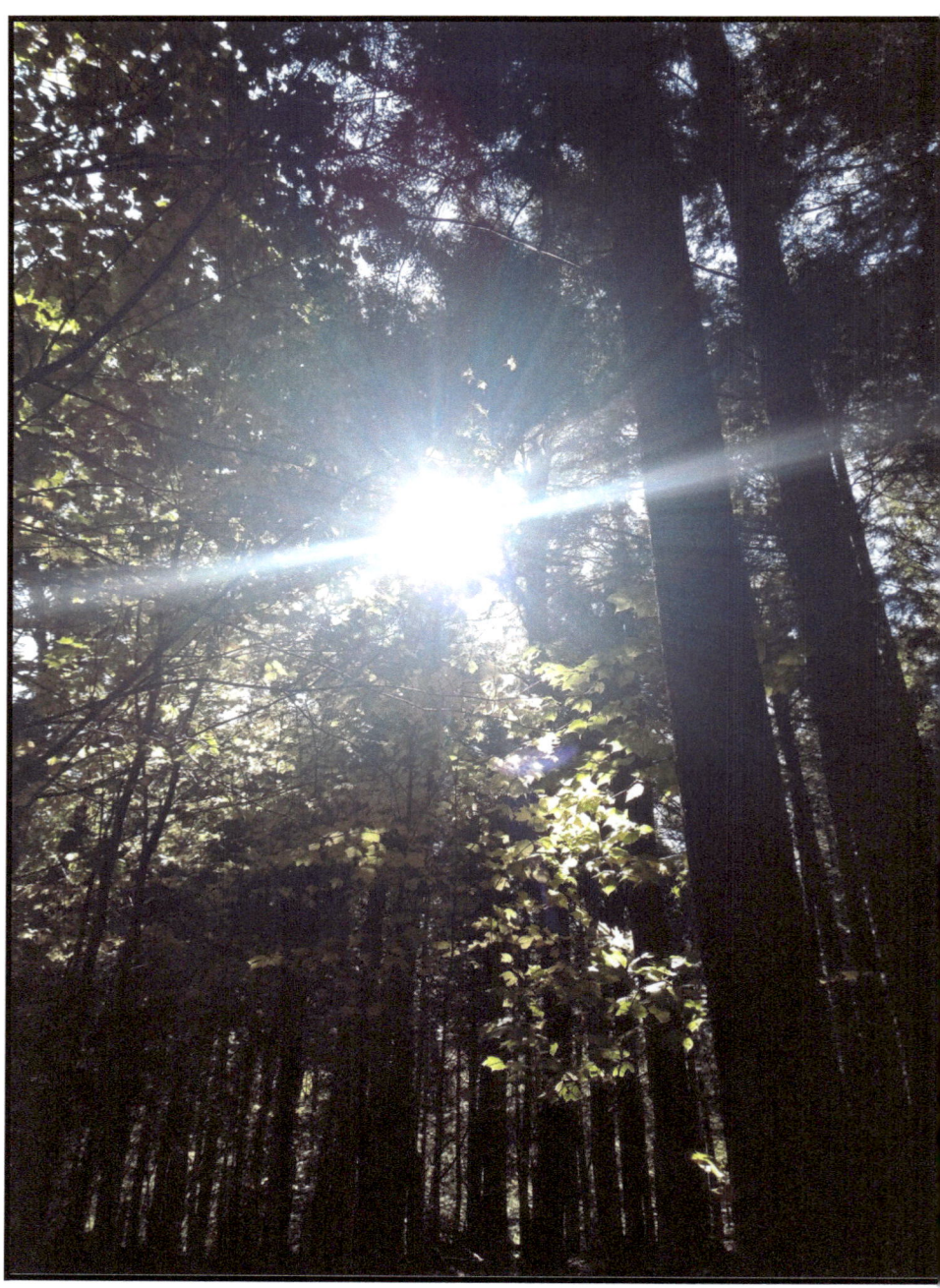

Image of You

Within jet astral sky of night
A Northeast point receives me true
The welcome mark of muse has passed
I know I've found my place with you.
Your poet's mystic soulful eyes
And words shall live through mine
In perfect love our handfast rites
Shall justify lost time.
No tool can smooth the edge I beg,
Depart not from this mirth,
Mere moments rest will die for sure
Inside this sleepless verse.
Watch me through those soulful eyes
My poet, pure insight,
The steps are slow but lead to you
The Godly root of life.

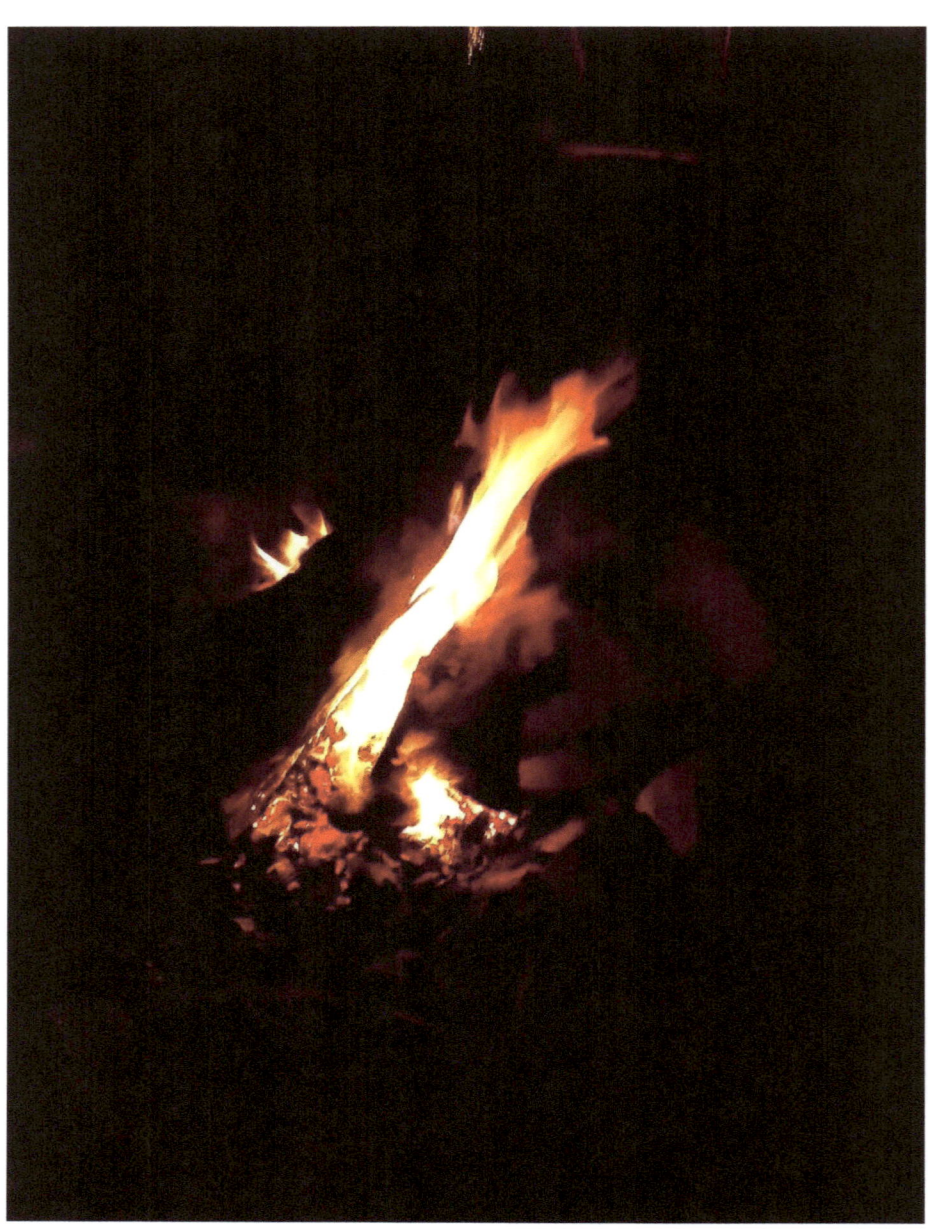

The Dance

Fly circles around my madness where
Shadows leap from substance
Divided, wild and dancing,
Spiral wings of one lash out,
Vicariously enhancing.
The night commences in sweetest grace
Commanding fire,
Relaxed and free,
Saddened shadows show their face,
They yearn to join
The Dance with me.
Golden tress flowing and warm,
Court the child,
Await the storm.
The night commences
In sweetest grace
Brilliant, wild and free,
Shadows embrace,
Take their rightful place
Joining storms to dance with me.

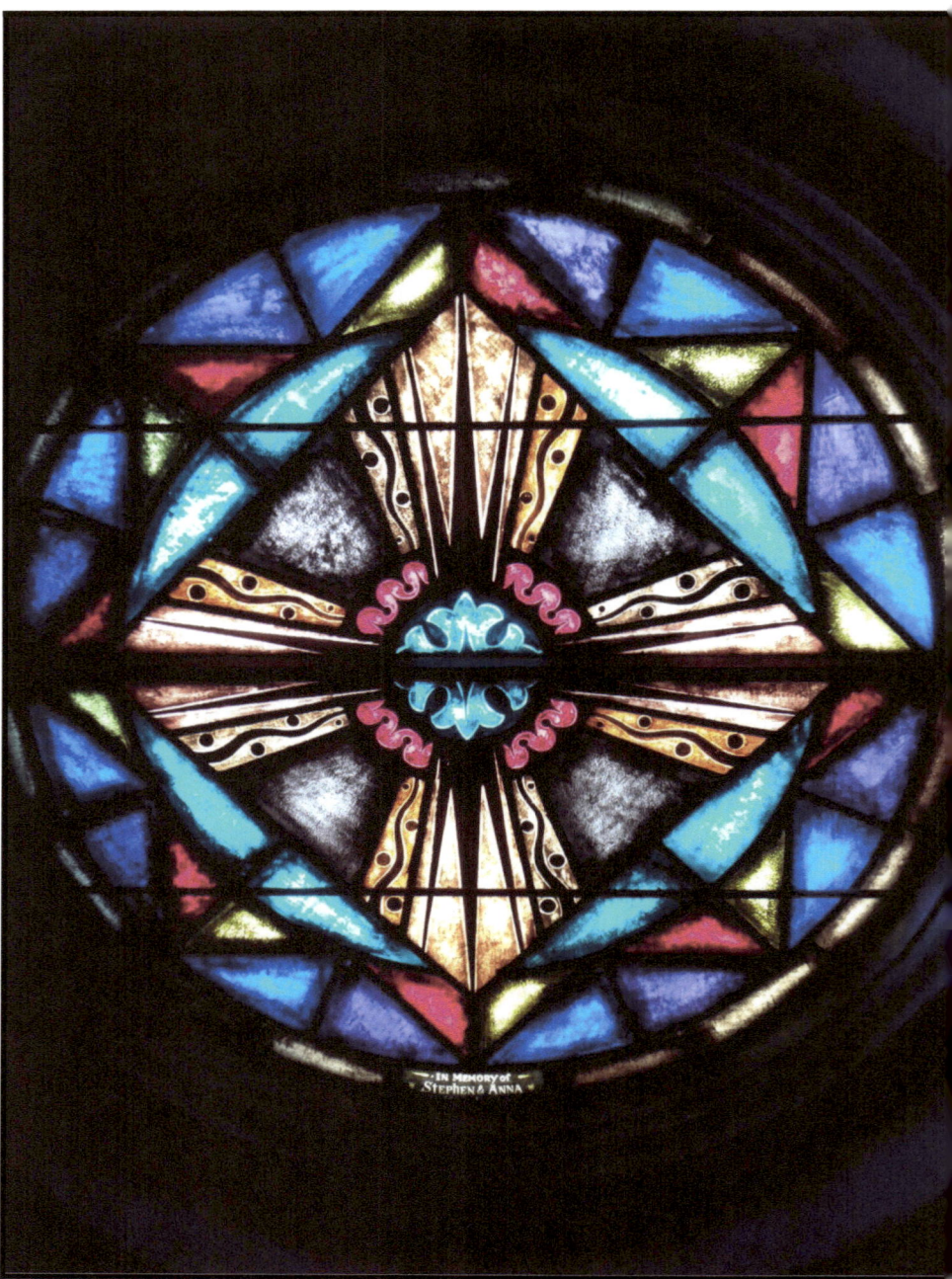

Poems of Damnation…The Seven Deadly Sinners

….Weep Not upon the weary pages of Ever After,
Thee will not find the answers there
Only the Author of broken souls can write their destinies…
Make them worthy enough to hear,
Bring light to darkness, see the tears
Innocent cries from innocent years
Stolen forever by cruel intent
Beyond forgiveness,
Their Punishment death…

SINNER #1

Not worthy of portrait nor photograph

You burn within the deepest circles of Hell…

Yes I can do this from above

Innocence never lies…it is mine and I reclaim it

Cradled within the broken shards of my soul

My Angel protects me now,

And raises my worth upon the highest Heavens

Where your sin nor soul can NEVER tread.

SINNER #2

Truth, Trust, Forever

Never

Love, Promise, Together

Never

Friendships Freedoms, Youth

Never

Dances, Parties, Places

Never

Distance, Distractions, Forgotten

OVER

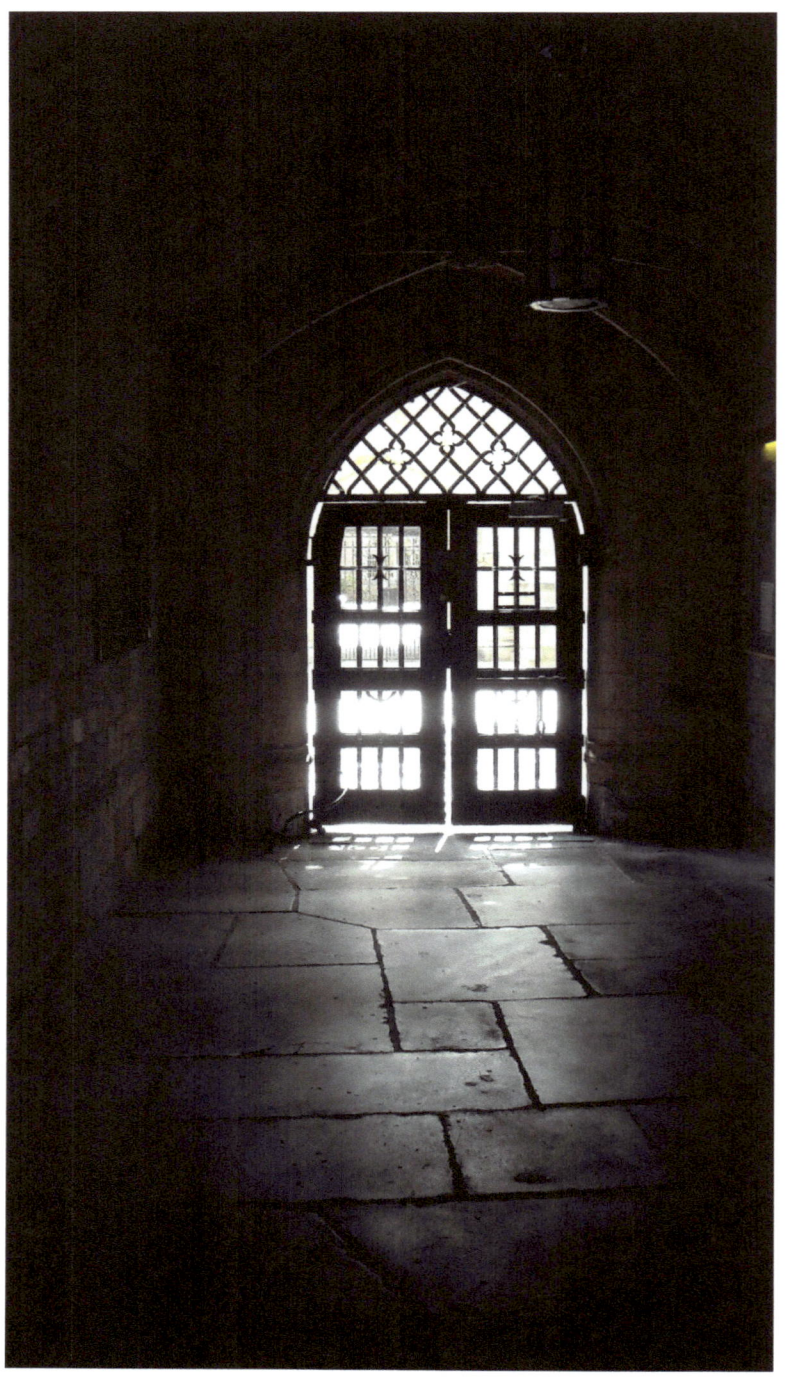

SINNER #3

Betrothed, Beloved
My partner forever
Wind in our hair
Ocean Spray
Lies, Infidelities,
Sinking to the Bottomless Sea
Where your sin and soul
Greet you for Eternity.

SINNER #4

Timeless…

Family carried up through the winds of change,

Casting souls apart and broken

Away from home,

Away from me

Where selfish acts are judged and tried

Where every word

Has been erased

Within the family bond

The only truth that remains

Is the Maternal devotion of

A Loving Mother to her Children.

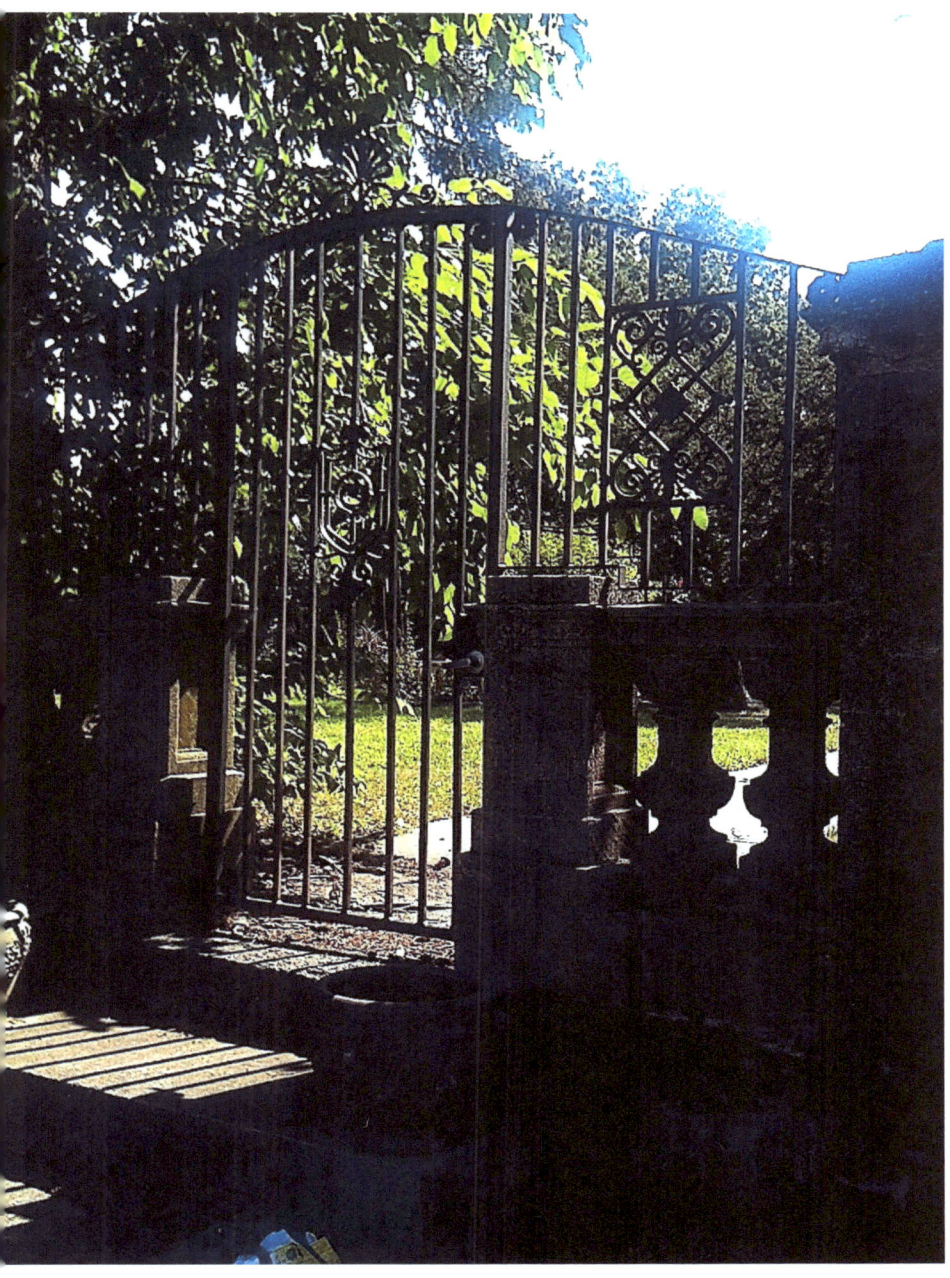

SINNER #5

Beautiful Darkness
Beautiful Love
What pages of life we did see
Nothing endearing
Nothing of me
Can ever come as eloquently
As the feeling of dread
Inescapable death
Bleeding, Foreboding
Love lost on a breathe
I'll find you dying within the page
Befitting a demon of shadow and rage.

SINNER #6

NARCISSIST, FALSE SELF, MASQUERADE, POISON, TRAUMA BONDS, SOULSTEALER, CRUEL

Unsuspecting, unaware

Darkness, Evil, Cruelest intent

Unheard of til now,

Newest creation walking in plain sight

Manipulating,

Hating and loving all the same

Hell hath rejected you

And thrust you here in this real life Purgatory

You are living Hell - the Worst Hell,

Any unsuspecting soul could easily mistake as human

But, alas,

Hatred bleeds from thine eyes

Shrouded in that mask you wear

Concealing your true self

Unleashed upon the world in all your fury

Only to be met by a Messenger

My purpose unknown until now

To stand between Darkness and Light

Removed from this Hell

And placed atop the highest thrones of Heaven

Ever powerful and Unyielding

And you Cast to the Deepest Tiers of Hell for Eternity.

SINNER #7

No Respect, No boundaries, Insanity,
Ghosted, as fitting as should be
You town crier you, with no divinity,
Nothing left for those to see,
Just an empty road to flee,
To shrug the cares off when in need,
The road stops here for all to see.

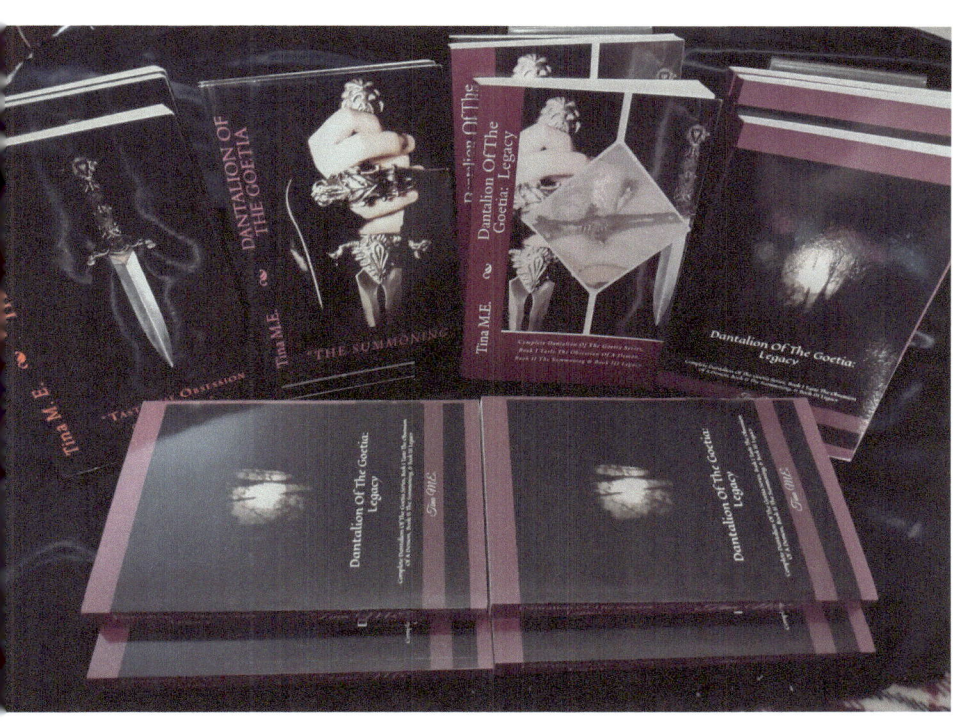

EPILOGUE
(To The Dantalion Of The Goetia Fantasy Fiction Series)

You called but I didn't hear, I continued searching
through the pages of history for the answers.
My gateway to memories, my visions of the past, cast from the sea
and to the forest grove to places I've seen through my ancestors,
the ones who came before. Answers for my journey and place among
the Angels of Heaven and the sins of Hell.

I found the writing of my father's hand,
heart broken musings of a half-demon.
I, Magzinnia, born a wisp, half-fairy and half-witch
who led him to his madness, now finding my own fate, here,
where I too, do not belong to this place beyond Heaven nor Hell.

I discovered my dark hair and eyes
were that of my father, Rowan,
who loved her so madly he brandished an elixir from the frozen ice,
if only to touch upon her memories. I too saw the memories.
I saw them every waking moment of my life,
never letting me be free of them.

The demons who built up the realm
to honor Dantalion and Laurel,
and their Legacy, never quite finishing the writing of their own destinies,
yet still, calling me through the veil to the ancient oak and stone,
marking the trail of their forgotten realm…

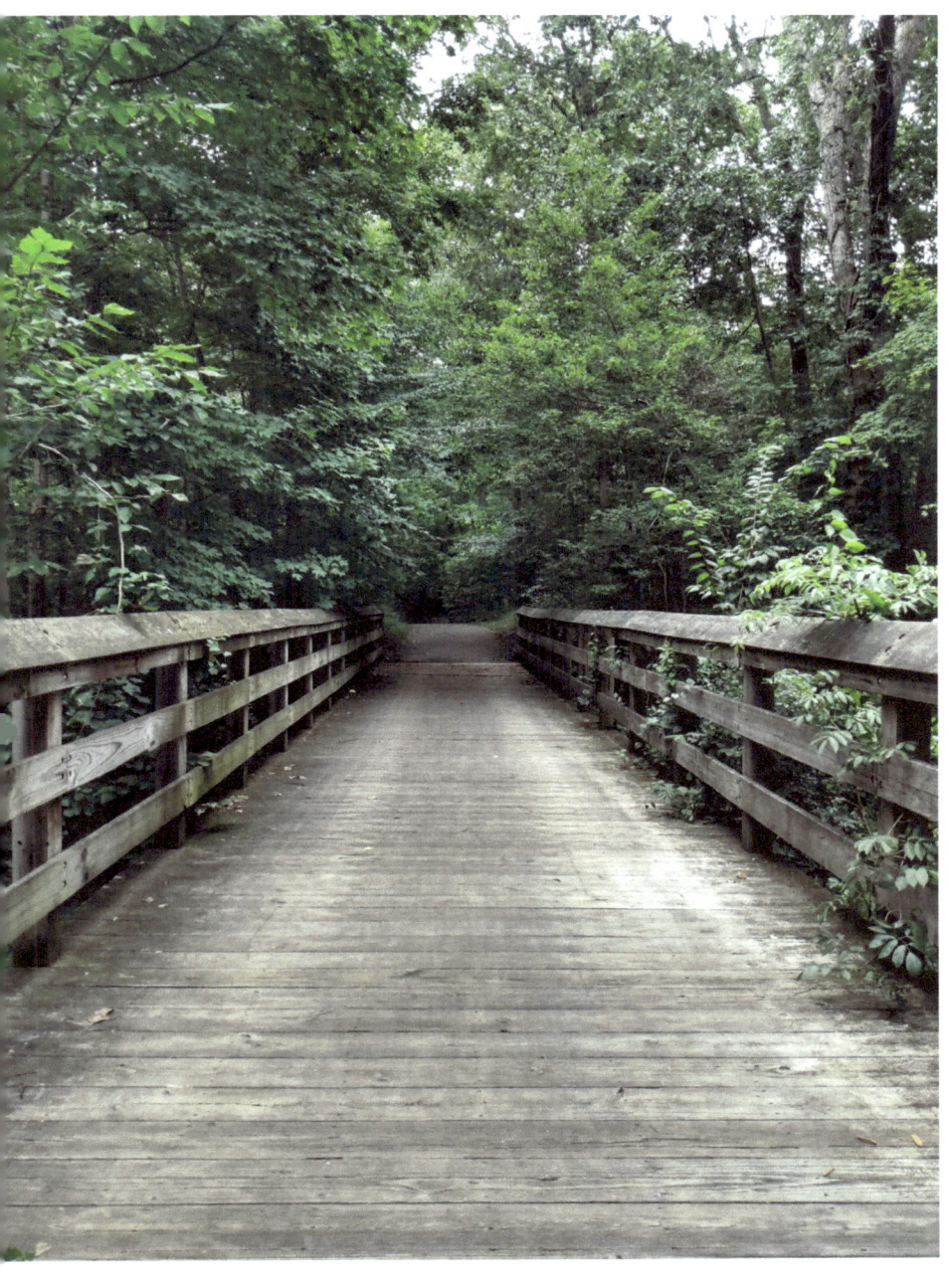

AFTERWARD

The Many Masks of Magzinnia has been a long awaited untold collection of writings of Poetry and musings, tying together the delicate threads of destiny. The destinies and Judgement of the seven Deadly Sinners who have been cast Down into the Darkest Hells for all Eternity, and the destiny of what is left of my life as a Holy Witch, neither of Heaven nor of Hell, but working towards Heaven. The poems tell stories of darkness and the severing of trauma bonds, as well as emerging one's soul back into the light.

The characters of my Dark Fantasy Series Dantalion Of The Goetia have a large impact on the writings in The Many Masks of Magzinnia. She is the final descendent of one of the main characters of the Dantalion Series, and only Magzinnia can choose to bring them back to life, whether It be in body or in spirit. She is forever the keeper of all our destinies, and only she wears the Mask of Mercy. Her name was created by my youngest daughter, both of them having that childlike innocence And certainty, and knowing forever they are the storytellers, the Creators, the keepers of secrets and the messengers of Justice.

She goes by many faces, many masks
Twirling, dancing movements in Autumn's whimsical canvas,
Childlike, fresh and untainted by the torments of humanity,
The beating down of one's Soul by the familiar and unfamiliar alike,
No, you sweet Magzinnia,
You wear the Mask of Mercy.

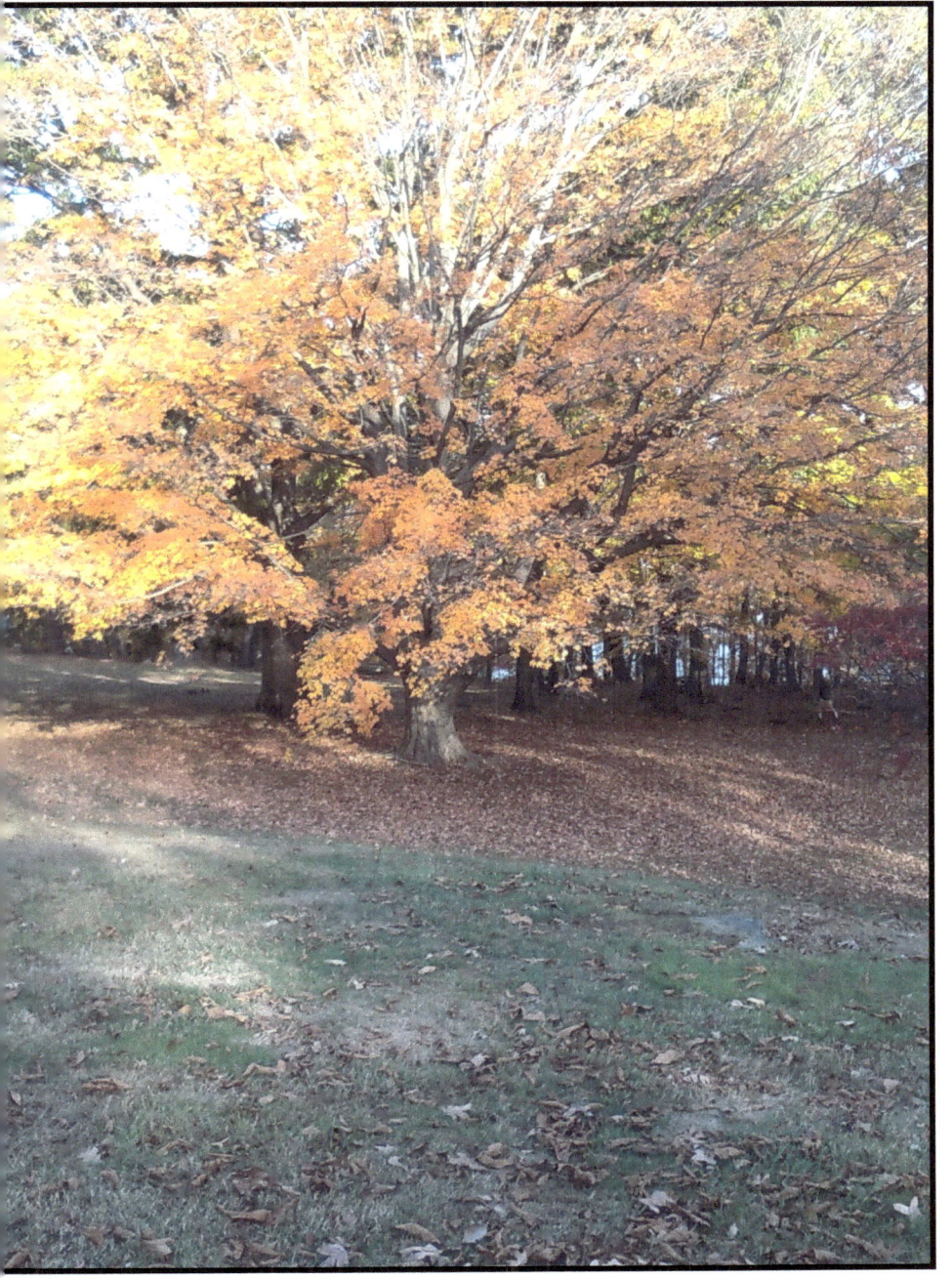

Author's Note:

" My soul is ancient, so I must heal from within,
My heart is pure so I must bleed alone."

About The Author:

Tina M. E. is Author of Dantalion Of The Goetia Dark Fantasy Series, The Silent Serenade, Tiny House Tale, The Many Masks of Magzinnia, Recipient of Editor's Choice Award for Outstanding Achievements in Poetry, journalist, screenwriter, advocate for young adult writers in her community, and long time follower of the Tiny House Movement And all things whimsical.

FOLLOW THE AUTHOR TINA M.E.

www.tinyindiewhimsy.com
www.instagram.com/tinyindiewhimsy
www.goodreads.com/dantalionofthegoetia
www.tiktok.com/demondarkfantasy
www.youtube.com/demondarkfantasy

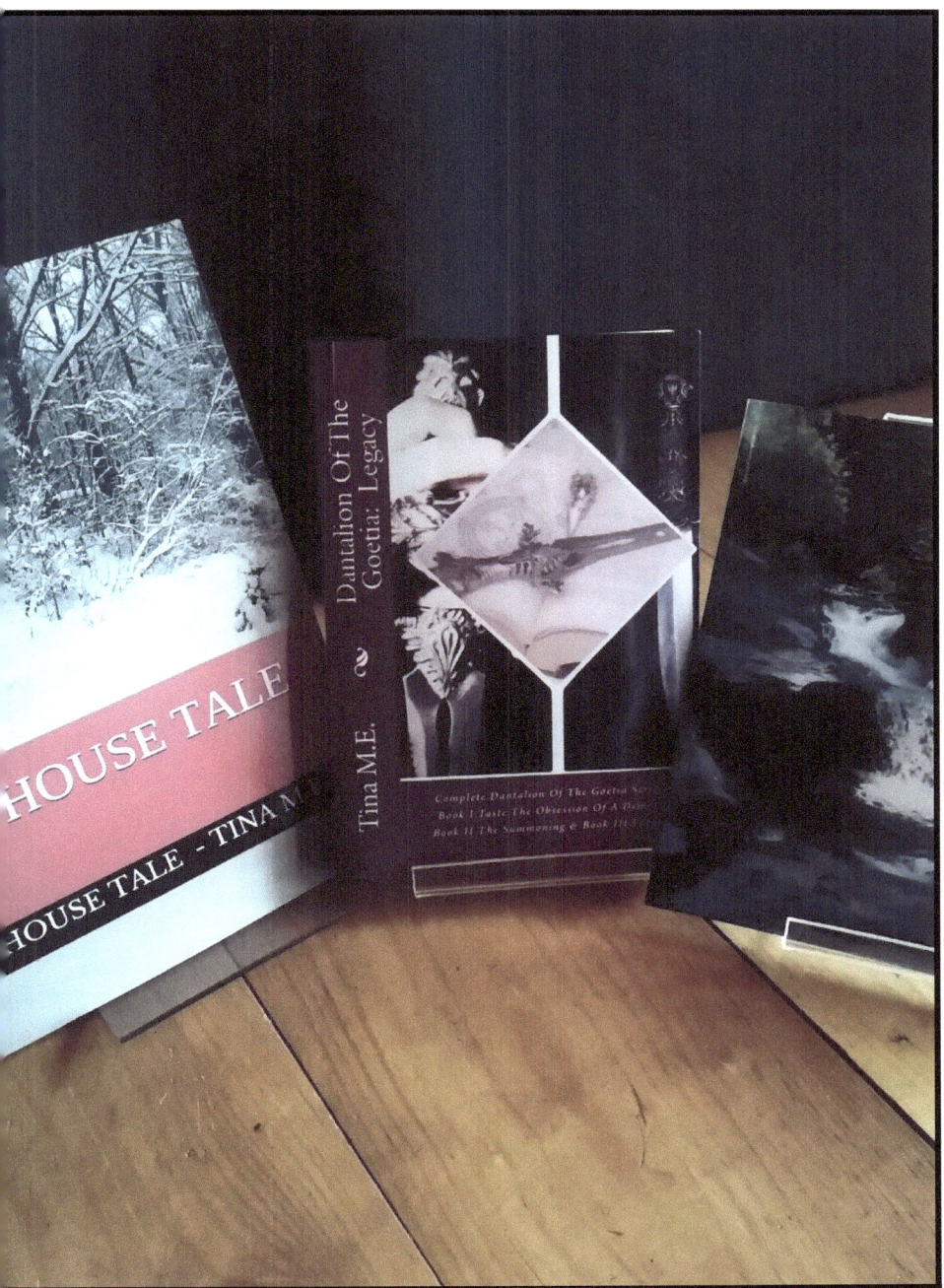

www.ingramcontent.com/pod-product-compliance
Lightning Source LLC
Chambersburg PA
CBHW040248220526
45473CB00001B/413